3,8

740L

PEACHTREE CITY LIBRARY
201 Willowbend Road
Peachtree City, GA 30269-1623
Phone: 770-631-2520
Fax: 770-631-2522

DANICA PATRICK

by Connie Colwell Miller

Printed in the United States of America,
North Mankato, Minnesota
102012
012013

 THIS BOOK CONTAINS AT LEAST 10% RECYCLED MATERIALS.

Editor: Chrös McDougall
Series Designer: Becky Daum

Photo Credits: Autostock/Nigel Kinrade/AP Images, cover, title; Cal Sport Media/AP Images, cover, 26, 27, 30 (bottom); Katsumi Kasahara/AP Images, 4-5, 6, 7; Shuji Kajiyama/AP Images, 8, 9, 22-23, 30 (top), 31; Brainerd Daily Dispatch/Clint Wood/AP Images, 10-11; The Janesville Gazette/Lukas Keapproth/AP Images, 12-13; Marcio Jose Sanchez/AP Images, 14-15; Mark J. Terrill/AP Images, 16-17; Michael Conroy/AP Images, 18; Darron Cummings/AP Images, 19, 30 (center); Tom Strickland/AP Images, 20-21; Dave Martin/AP Images, 24-25; George Tiedemann/GT Images/Corbis/AP Images, 28-29

Cataloging-in-Publication Data
Colwell Miller, Connie.
 Danica Patrick / Connie Colwell Miller.
   p. cm. -- (NASCAR heroes)
Includes bibliographical references and index.
ISBN 978-1-61783-666-4
1. Patrick, Danica, 1982- --Juvenile literature. 2. Automobile racing drivers--United States--Biography--Juvenile literature. 3. Women automobile racing drivers--United States--Biography--Juvenile literature. I. Title.
796.72092--dc21
 [B]

2012946334

CONTENTS

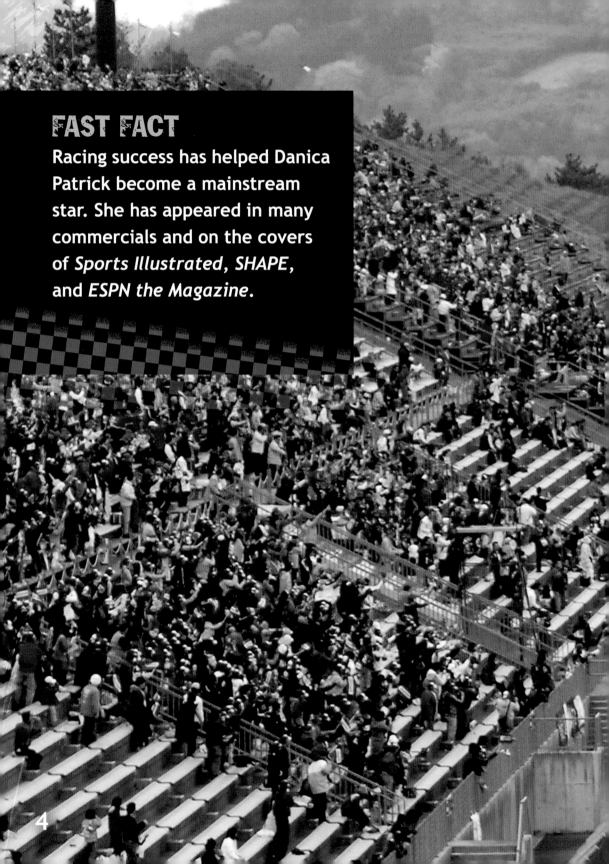

FAST FACT

Racing success has helped Danica Patrick become a mainstream star. She has appeared in many commercials and on the covers of *Sports Illustrated*, *SHAPE*, and *ESPN the Magazine*.

A BIG WIN

Only five laps remained in the 2008 Indy Japan 300. Driver Danica Patrick was keeping pace with the pack in the IndyCar race. But for Patrick, keeping pace wasn't good enough. She wanted the win.

The 2008 Indy Japan 300 IndyCar race in Motegi, Japan

Patrick goes through Turn 4 at the 2008 Indy Japan 300.

Suddenly, the leading driver was forced to pit. Two other drivers stopped for gas. With two laps left, it was down to Patrick and one other driver.

The other driver's fuel supply was low. He began to sputter out. Patrick sped on, leaving him in the dust. She crossed the finish line first.

Patrick kisses her husband Paul Hospenthal after winning the 2008 Indy Japan 300.

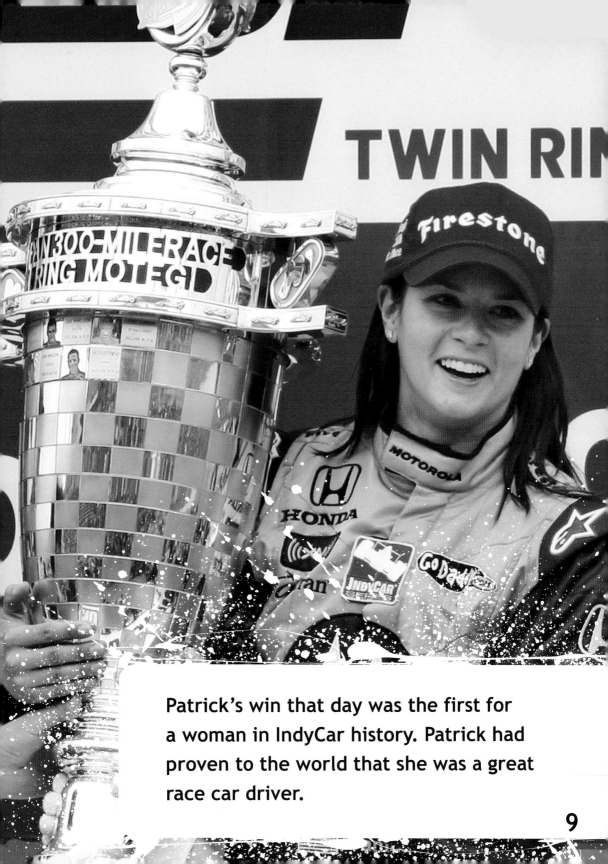

Patrick's win that day was the first for a woman in IndyCar history. Patrick had proven to the world that she was a great race car driver.

A WINNING SPIRIT

Danica Sue Patrick was born on March 25, 1982, in Beloit, Wisconsin. She grew up in Illinois. When Danica was young, her father raced snowmobiles. More than anything, Danica and her younger sister Brooke wanted to race like their father.

Danica wanted to race snowmobiles like her dad when she was growing up.

The girls begged to race. Finally, their parents bought the girls go-karts. When Danica was 10 years old, she and her sister began racing go-karts. Danica's sister soon gave up racing. Danica never did.

Like many young racers,
Danica first raced go-karts.

Patrick found her calling racing open-wheel cars and IndyCars.

STARTING IN INDY

Patrick won many go-kart races. Before long she was ready for a bigger challenge. At age 16, she moved to England to learn to race open-wheel cars.

FAST FACT

Danica Patrick raced in the Formula Ford Festival in England in 2000. There, she achieved the highest finish by any US race car driver.

In England, Patrick's drive to win grew even stronger. Her toughness on the track caught the eye of IndyCar racing team owner Bobby Rahal. He invited Patrick to race in the United States in 2002. Patrick started out in small races. By 2003, she was competing in tougher and tougher races for the Rahal Letterman Racing team. It is now called Rahal Letterman Lanigan Racing.

In 2005, Patrick was ready to race with the best of the best in IndyCar racing. She was ready for the Indy Racing League (IRL).

FAST FACT

Bobby Rahal co-owns the Rahal Letterman Lanigan Racing team with comedian David Letterman and Mike Lanigan. Letterman hosts the *Late Show with David Letterman* on CBS.

Patrick heads down the straightaway at a 2002 sports car race.

FAST FACT

Danica Patrick was
the fourth woman
to race in the
Indianapolis 500.

*Patrick and her crew
practice a pit stop before
the 2005 Indianapolis 500.*

BREAKING RECORDS

Patrick raced in the Indianapolis 500 in 2005. She had been dreaming of competing in that famous race since she was a girl. And she did more than just compete. Patrick finished fourth. That was the best finish for any female driver in the history of the Indianapolis 500. That same year, the IRL named Patrick Rookie of the Year.

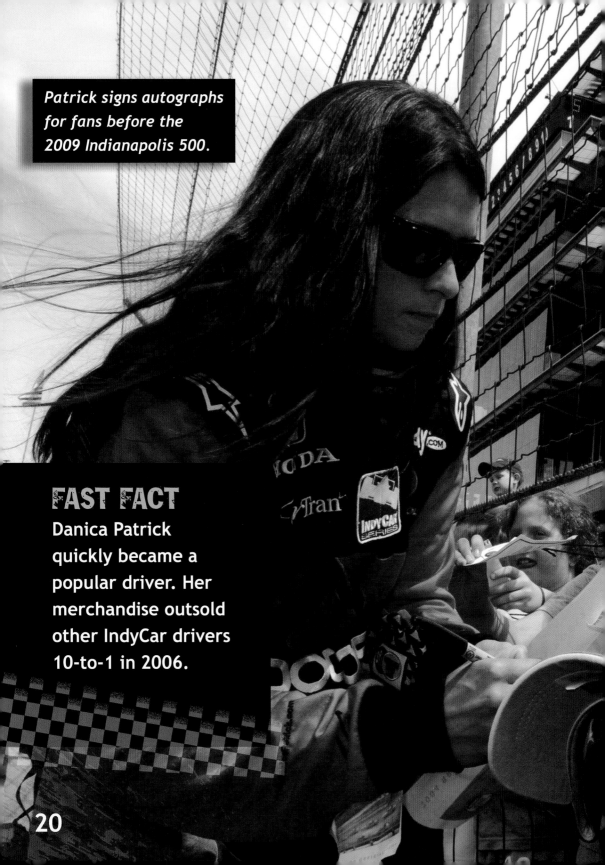

Patrick signs autographs for fans before the 2009 Indianapolis 500.

FAST FACT

Danica Patrick quickly became a popular driver. Her merchandise outsold other IndyCar drivers 10-to-1 in 2006.

Patrick continued having success in IndyCar racing. In 2008, she won her first IndyCar race in Japan. Then, in 2009, she came in third at the Indianapolis 500. She beat her own record.

FAST FACT

Besides both having four wheels, stock cars and IndyCars have few similarities. For example, IndyCars can go up to 230 miles per hour (370 km/h) while stock cars max out around 200 mph (322 km/h).

MOVING TO NASCAR

IndyCar fans everywhere began to see Patrick as a tough and strong-willed competitor. The National Association for Stock Car Auto Racing (NASCAR) owners noticed, too. They asked her to join their teams. But Patrick only wanted to race IndyCars.

Patrick stuck with IndyCars in 2009.

Finally, in 2010, Patrick joined NASCAR. That year, she raced in 13 Nationwide Series races. Patrick saw improvement the next year. She finished fourth at the Sam's Town 300. That was the best finish of any woman ever in NASCAR.

In her first years of NASCAR racing, Patrick raced in IndyCar, too. In 2012, Patrick committed full-time to NASCAR.

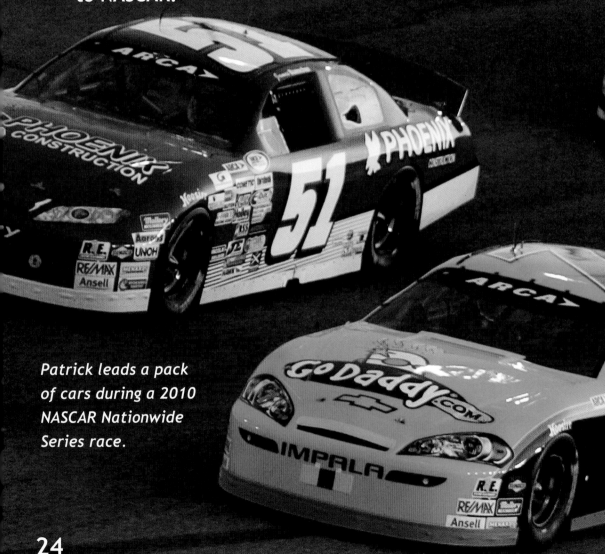

Patrick leads a pack of cars during a 2010 NASCAR Nationwide Series race.

GREATEST ACCOMPLISHMENTS

Patrick has proven to be a competitive driver in both IndyCar and NASCAR racing. But she has achieved another kind of victory altogether. Patrick has dominated in a sport with mostly male competitors. She has become a role model for female athletes everywhere.

Patrick had one top-five finish in the Nationwide Series in 2011.

Patrick leads the pack at a 2012 Nationwide Series race at Daytona International Speedway.

Patrick continues to race in NASCAR full-time. In 2012, she began racing in the top-level Sprint Cup Series in addition to the Nationwide Series. She even raced in the famous Daytona 500 that year. Only time will tell what else the future has in store for Danica Patrick.

TIMELINE

1982

Danica Sue Patrick is born on March 25 in Beloit, Wisconsin.

1998

Patrick moves to England to race open-wheel cars.

2005

Patrick marries physical therapist Paul Hospenthal.

2005

Patrick places fourth in the Indianapolis 500.

2008

Patrick wins her first IndyCar race.

2009

Patrick places third in the Indianapolis 500.

2010

Patrick makes her NASCAR debut.

2012

Patrick begins racing in NASCAR's Sprint Cup Series.

GLOSSARY

crew
The people who service a race car.

IndyCar
A type of race car with one seat and open wheels without frames around them.

Nationwide Series
NASCAR's second-level series for professional stock car drivers.

owner
The person who owns an entire racing team. This person hires everyone on the team, including the driver and the crew.

pit
When a driver enters the pit area for service on his or her vehicle.

rookie
A driver in his or her first full-time season in a new series.

Sprint Cup Series
NASCAR's top series for professional stock car drivers.

stock car
Race cars that resemble models of cars that people drive every day.

INDEX